HOW TO WAIT
&
GET THE RIGHT PARTNER

(FOR BACHELORS & SPINSTERS)

ESTHER ATOI

Contents

DEDICATION

I dedicate this book to God Almighty who gave me the talent, gifts and Inspiration to write this book through the help of the Holy Spirit.
God sustains my life through his word as a lamp to my feet to witness this work come to reality so that I can be fulfilled and he is glorified.

I give him all the Glory!

ACKNOWLEDGEMENTS

First, I acknowledge God, my helper who has been seeing me through all my endeavors. I'm forever grateful.

I appreciate my Mum and my Siblings for their love and support,
I will not forget to thank my husband, Mr Tony Atoi for being there for me.

Thanks to my coach, Dr Eunice Iwuala for coming when I needed someone to show me the way out in publishing this book. She is God-sent.

Finally, I also want to appreciate all the readers of this book, especially the Waiting Singles; God loves you and has not forgotten you!

INTRODUCTION

This book explains the meaning of the waiting period. It analyses some things bachelors and Spinsters should know before they get married and opens your eyes to understand your waiting process, causes of delay in marriage and solutions.

This book elaborates on what you must know in the time of waiting or delay and what you should do as a way of taking action with faith in God to avoid unnecessary hindrances to getting the right partner.

This book will help you know what God expects from you when you are passing through unpleasant moments and avoid worry and anxiety but highlights what to do on your part instead to pass the test of time because you must pass the test before you can move to the next level.

You will also learn three important roles involved in a waiting period, your part and God's part to have wonderful testimonies.

This book is loaded with many life experiences from the Author and other people and how to prepare for your awaiting wife or husband.

It also contains biblical examples of those who passed the test during their waiting period with some strategies you can adopt too and much more.

Finally, it contains practical testimonies about the Author when she was a spinster. This will help the faith of everyone in any difficult situations by his Grace.

CHAPTER ONE

WHAT IS THE WAITING PERIOD?

For the Singles waiting for marriage, the waiting period is a period when a Spinster is praying and waiting for God for her future husband or when a Bachelor is still searching for his future wife.

A waiting period is also a time you wait for your miracle or blessing to manifest physically.

A waiting period is an inevitable moment in your life when God allows you to have some training experiences that can make you strong and fulfil your purpose in life. It is God's process, and it differs from satanic delay or manipulations.

It is a period of praying and waiting for God to do a new thing in your life or for God to show up quickly in your

situation but God seems to be silent or slow to act.
This is a period you are expecting something to show for your request from God but unknown to you, God is working it out spiritually but you are yet to see the manifestation.

You may not like the experience; it is not a period to kill you but to make you because it is a process of God to take you to your promised land. No matter what the enemies may do, God will still change it for good, like in the story of Joseph.

It is a period that I can describe as a horrible pit and miry clay.

*"I **waited patiently for the Lord, and he inclined unto me, and heard my cry,***
He brought me up also out of a horrible pit, out of the miry clay; and

set my feet upon a rock, and establish my goings"
(Psalm40 v 1-2).KJV.

According to the above scripture, the Psalmist says two things that are keywords:

"Waited Patiently."

First, what does it mean **to wait?** Second, how can we **be patient** in our waiting?
This makes me understand that; some people can wait in anxiety, sin, desperation, bitterness, ignorance, laziness and anger instead of waiting patiently in faith, Joy, love, expectation and preparations.
As a bachelor or Spinster, you must see 'waiting' as your preparatory program to be a good husband or wife to your awaiting spouse.

The psalmist says **"I waited"**.

I will also describe waiting as a period
when you experience a delay in
answered prayer.
The followings are some of the things
you should know about your waiting:

• A waiting period is a period of
testing your love for God.
• It is a period of trial.
• It is a period of self-examination.
• It is a time God tests your faith in
him.
• It is time you endure hardship before
victory.
• It is a time of expectation from God.
• A waiting period is a period of
training for you.
• It is a period of brokenness in all
areas of your life to allow God to exalt
you in due season.
• It is a period of teaching and learning
what God wants you to learn.
• It is a time of preparation for God to
equip you to be who he wants you to
become.

• It is a period that God is recording your maturity and readiness for his blessing.
• It may be an unpleasant time before any miracle or victory.
• It is a period you wait on God and also do some remarkable things for his kingdom before the testimony.
• It is a time to build yourself up in all areas.
• A waiting period is a learning period.
• It is a time to receive corrections and improve your character.
• The waiting period has wilderness experiences.

In the same (Psalm 40 v 1a) says I waited **"Patiently"**
"To wait patiently" means
• The time of your waiting on God must be total.
• It means to wait on God without fear.
• It means to wait on God without compromise.

• To wait on God without a doubt in your mind.
• It means to wait without anxiety or worry.
• It means you must believe and trust in God to give you a good thing.
• It means you must not find another alternative to God or to what he promises to give you.
• It shows your totality, preparation and endurance to receive from God.
• Patience is the price for waiting on God. Can you pay the price?
• There is power in waiting.
• Waiting patiently is waiting faithfully.

CHAPTER TWO

REASONS FOR WAITING PERIOD

There are many reasons we may experience delays or waiting periods, this is because as a believer in the word of God,

"All things work together for our good."

While we are in a waiting period, God wants us to pass through some training and until we learn, accept, obey and prepare to do what God expects us to do; things may not fall in shape. Sometimes, the reasons you experience a waiting period may be:

1. God wants to show his Glory:

You may have a delay in some areas because God wants to glorify His name and marvellous work through you. So it may not be that you are a sinner but he just wants to make something great out of your situation so that you know he is God.

2. **To get rid of certain behaviour.**
(Galatians 5 v 19–21)

"Now the works of the flesh are manifest, which are these; Adultery, fornication, uncleanness, lasciviousness, Idolatry, witchcraft, hatred, variance, emulations, wrath, strife, seditions, heresies, Envying, murders, drunkenness, reveling, and such like: of the which I tell you before, as I have also told you in time past, that they which do such things shall not inherit the kingdom of God".
Many times we lose some miracles because we cannot resist the temptations that want to hinder our miracle. Trace any flaw in your life and deal with it, Satan is using it repeatedly through people around you

to deprive you of your blessing. It can be anger, bitterness, unforgiving heart, hatred, sorrow or pride? All these are the work of the flesh.

3. To learn certain things from your situation and to equip you with necessary spiritual virtues: (Galatians 5 v 22- 26)

**"But the fruit of the Spirit is love, joy, peace, long-suffering, gentleness, goodness, faith, Meekness, temperance: against such there is no law,
If we live in the Spirit, let us also walk in the spirit.
Let us not be desirous of vain glory, provoking one another, envying one another."**

Waiting is necessary for you to experience emotional maturity, spiritual maturity, and growth in the word of God, prayers, faith and Godly characters.

You must discover what you lack in your life to overcome.
Get some physical and spiritual training, Learn, get equipped and prepare for your blessing.

A waiting period is a training period!
A waiting period is a learning period!!
A waiting period is a preparation period!!!!
A waiting period is an examination period!!!

BIBLE EXAMPLES OF PEOPLE WHO EXPERIENCE TRAINING, LEARNING & PREPARATION IN THEIR WAITING PERIOD.

Without faith, we cannot please God, and faith without action is dead.

The following are biblical Examples of people with faith and actions in their waiting period:-

(1). David - (Samuel, chapter 17). David did not just become a king overnight without a price; God trained him in the field to tend sheep. As young as he was, he knew God; he trusted in God, and he knew how to lead his sheep in the bush, he was a good shepherd. He was also a warrior and he could tear a lion in the bush, so it was not a surprise to him he could kill Goliath. All the battles he encountered when he was nobody, formed a training for him in the wilderness and made him strong enough to fight a giant that was molesting his people. What is that situation that represents a giant in your life? Is it a Delay in marriage? Joblessness? Poverty? Whatever it may be, God is using your situation in training or preparing you for a greater Glory. Make the best of this situation, you may say it from Satan, yes that is why you need to pray till your joy is full but God is aware of what is happening. If you are on God's side, he will fight for you.

Despite all the discouragement and distraction from David's brothers, he knew God and went after the giant. What happened? He **conquered.** How about you? Do you know God? Are you faithful in your service to him? God may train you as a prayer warrior, a Prophet, and a High minister, you must discover who you are by seeking God more in prayer.

(2). The Children of Israel–(Number 13: 25–33).

God tested the Israelites in the wilderness at the water of Meribah before they entered the Promised Land.

God also tested their trust in him when they went to spy on the land and saw the giants. Caleb and Joshua believed in God and his deliverance and as a result, possessed the Promised Land. God is still watching us see those who believe in him in all situations, no matter how terrible, God can still fix it. God destroyed all the people that doubted him.

If God wants to give you a million, he may test you with a thousand to see how wise you can manage it. If you fail; you may have to repeat the test till you have learnt a lesson, so you will not mess up the bigger opportunities he will bring to you.

(3) Adam: - Genesis 2 v 19.

"And out of the ground, the Lord formed every beast of the field, and every fowl of the air and brought them to Adam to see what he would call them: and whatsoever Adam called every living creature that was the name thereof."

God tested Adam to see the name he would call the animals, he could have called one animal, his Wife, but none of the animals could fit as his companion. Adam gave names to all the animals, but he could not find help-meet among the animals and had to wait for his wife from God and not among the animals that were keeping his company. Then God saw his need and provided him with a helpmeet, **Eve**, the bone of his bone and the flesh of his flesh. (Reference: Genesis 2v 18 -23) KJV.

(4).Abraham:- Genesis 22 v 1-14.
Abraham was qualified as a father of faith for his price of obedience, love, trust and faithfulness to God; he was ready to sacrifice his promised child, (Isaac) to God.
What are you ready to let go of for God? Even though God will not ask you to kill your child for him again

because Jesus Christ has settled that for us on the cross for the atonement of our sin and redemption, can you sacrifice your time for him in evangelism, reading and meditation of his word?
Prayer and intercession? What about your gift and talent?

(5).Ruth:- (Ruth chapter 3 & 4)
Ruth was a dedicated woman who focused and trusted in the God of Israel. What happened after her dedication to God was a testimony of marriage, fruitfulness and abundance. Are you a Spinster, bachelor, widow or single mum? You can learn from the dedication of Ruth and trust God to get to a new level.

(6) Queen Esther: -. (Esther 2 v 1-18)
Before they crowned Esther as a queen, she passed through physical

and spiritual training. After that, she was also ready to put down her life to save her people. Can God trust you to be a vehicle of salvation and deliverance to your family? Can you fast for them? Can you intercede in prayer for others? If you must rise as a queen, God must equip you. Therefore, learn what you have to learn, pass through the training in test and prepare for the opportunity.

How much of the word of God do you meditate and obey?

In conclusion, God also has his timing in your waiting period, so you should discern the time and he expects you to fulfil your part. You need to pray for his help and mercy as you take some necessary actions.

There are some steps of faith we need to take for faith to manifest in our lives.

Therefore,
get **wisdom, Knowledge, Understand
ing** and **Revelation of his word** as you
take **necessary actions** with **faith** in
your heart.

CHAPTER THREE

WHAT TO LEARN IN THE WAITING PERIOD

God allows a waiting period for you to learn, observe and guard against certain things in your life. God loves you but he can permit a waiting period to correct you by allowing some situations to happen for a reason that he knows you can overcome.
He does not hate you, and he has not forsaken you but he may train you, for instance, as a young preacher, a counsellor, as a financier to handle money wisely, because if you are faithful in little, he will give you more. God wants you to be wise, strong and also to observe:-

What to Learn and do during your waiting

1. Learn to be patient- (Luke 21 v 19, James 5 v 8).
2. Learn to be humble- (Proverb 15:33).
3. To be more prayerful- (1 Thessalonians 5:17).
4. Learn to guard your mouth– (Proverb 14:3, 12:14, 10:31-32 & 10:19, 4:24, 10:13, James 3:2).
5. To be mature enough to manage the blessing wisely.
6. To learn from your mistake or the mistake of others and avoid making another one.
7. To realize the task or challenge ahead of you and prepare for it– (Numbers 33:52-53).
8. In your waiting process, God may want to remove obstacles or enemies before you-(Joshua 3:10).
9. To Learn to pray to equip yourself with necessary weapons.
10. To learn how to trust God that delay is not denial-(Psalm21:7, 22: 4).

11. To know that you are in your making, as a queen like Esther or a king like David, your throne is waiting for you as you pass through the training.

12. If you have an unpleasant experience, it is a track record for you to counsel others who are in the same situation that God is faithful, he will fulfil his promises the way he fulfilled them in your life- (1st Timothy 6 v 12).

13. God may be waiting for you to know that it is not by your power so that you can surrender to him.

14. God may want to show his power through you- (Joshua 8: 1, act1: 8).

15. For you to learn to be joyful and thankful to God even in an unpleasant situation-(1st Thessalonica 5:16).

16. To test our faithfulness because there is always a test during the waiting period–(Genesis 39: 7-9).

17. Your waiting period is a signal that your testimony will be great.

18. He wants you to learn to meditate on the word of God-(Joshua1: 8, proverb 4: 14).

19. To discover and develop your gift, talent or potential.

20. To seek or get knowledge and wisdom about the vision of God in your life- (Proverb 4 v 7, 23 v 12).

21. Waiting period is a time to prepare and upgrade yourself in all areas- (Proverb 23v23).

22. To build your faith in God– (Hebrew 11v 1-40).

<u>Things not to do in the waiting period</u>

1. While you are awaiting your miracles, do not be idle in service to God.

2. Do not relent in prayer.

3. Do not complain, grumble or murmur against God.

4. Do not sin.

5. Do not gossip, backbite or become a busybody.
6. Do not be moody or sorrowful.
7. Do not envy others- (James 3:16).
8. Do not hold grudges in your heart.
9. Do not be careless with your life.
10. Do not think evil or become bitter.
11. Do not stop reading and meditating on the word of God.
12. Do not outrun God.
13. Do not doubt the promises of God.
14. Avoid sex before marriage.

CHAPTER FOUR

ESTHER'S PREPARATION

Preparation is the action you take for something to happen or it means getting ready for an event.
I want to use the scripture that helped me to illustrate some points from the story of Queen Esther who was nobody but because of the favour of God in her life and her preparation and obedience on her part became a queen. She could rise to the top.
According to (Esther 2 vs. 12) (NIV)

"Before a young woman's turn came to go into King Xerxes, she had to complete twelve months of beauty treatments prescribed for the women, six months with oil of myrrh and six months with perfumes and cosmetics."

From the latter part of the verse and the New International version, there are so many lessons we can learn from the story of Esther, chapter 2 verse 12 which says,

"6 months with oil of myrrh and 6 months of perfume and cosmetic, ": -

(1). **OIL OF MYRRH:** - The oil is a symbol of Anointing. When Esther was in her waiting period, she received an anointing to break every yoke. Anointing is very important in our lives, it also means receiving power from God to overcome temptation, sin, and trial, evil and above all, she received the guidance of the Holy Spirit for her preparation to become the queen. As a believer, you need the anointing, am not talking about physical oil, we all need the power of God to break every yoke that may form hindrances to the purpose of God for our lives. The bible says (Isaiah 10 v 27 b).

"And the yoke shall be destroyed because of the anointing"

The anointing is not just the oil but the power of God inside. We need to carry the power of God and we need the help of the Holy Spirit to guide us in our ways. Ask for the power of God, and ask for the Holy Spirit to work with you to fulfil your destiny.

(2). **PERFUME:** The perfume represents the strength or Grace of God to do his will. It also represents the favour of God, the Glory of God in your life. God gave Esther grace at this period to perform what she performed for her to be qualified as the next queen. You need the Grace of God and you need his divine favour to smell good for people to help you, just like Esther found favour with God and man. Pray for grace:

- To read, meditate and be a doer of the word of God,

-Grace to be 'where' God wants you to be
- Grace to be 'who' God wants you to be,
- You need the grace to do what God expects you to do.
- You need grace and strength from God during your waiting period to obey him fully.
- Pray for divine favour and flavour of God to smell good.

(3). **COSMETICS:** This represents our Christian virtues; Esther manifested the divine beauty of God with Godly characters.

As a Spinster, pray for the fruits of the Holy Spirit, wisdom, knowledge and understanding to be a virtuous woman (proverb 31:10-31), and let God know you are ready for marriage.

As a bachelor, position yourself to be an excellent man in character to rule over your home. You cannot give what you do not have, ask for the fruit of the Holy Spirit because, in the waiting period, you need wisdom, knowledge and understanding to move to the next level in life.

Many people in the bible passed through training, and they passed. For Esther, she replaced a Queen named Vashti.

An instruction was given to find a virgin, the king needed a woman of Godly character, virtues or a woman of better qualities, who is humble to replace the present queen because pride made queen Vashti fall, she disrespected the king's instruction (Esther 2vs.2-4).

The king's eunuch was in charge of the women's training affairs to give them ointment to pass through training, for them to prepare who will be fit to be the next Queen and Esther found favour with God and with man.

We can see that God put his favour upon Esther, yet she passed through some training. She prepared herself before the time; she did not misuse the Grace of God. God wanted her to be better than Vashti, Esther had to go for training, she was teachable and so she learnt, prepared and passed the test. Likewise, as children of God; born again, and sanctified we have to pass through some training in our challenges from time to time and it is better we learn on time so we do not delay ourselves. It was after Esther took the step to join in the training that she got good counsel (advice). She gained knowledge before the examination. (Esther 2 v 15).
Delay is not denial, God wants us to work out our mathematics well. He is waiting for you to do your part, do not be idle even if you have the grace of God or favour of God upon your life

and prepare for what you believe God for.

My Simple mathematics

1. Preparation + passed test = Favour
2. Favour + preparation = manifestation
3. Favour + idleness = Delay
4. Favour + preparation + passed test–idleness =wonderful testimony

The explanations of the above mathematics:

1. The first one means that before you experience favour, you need to prepare for something you are waiting for God to do, and then comes a test, you need the grace to pass it, it will come. For example, God may want to teach

you humility, Joy and other fruit of the Spirit, so get the message.

2. When your preparation meets the favour of God in your life, here comes the manifestation of the miracle of answered prayer. When you prepare, pray for the favour of God and your manifestation will come.

3. If the favour of God is in your life and you are idle, how will the favour be activated? If you wait in idleness or folding of hands, it will amount to delay, which is self-delay, this one is not from Satan but from you. Do your part and God will not fail his part.

4. The fourth one is the same as number one when you are not idle but prepared and you pass the test, then you experience wonderful testimonies.

God is always there to help us, provided you are teachable to learn, prepare, and work.

In the waiting period, there are two principal players involved: (You and God) you must perform your part. God can strengthen you, encourage, enlighten, instruct and raise people to help you. God is working for your good but you must refuse to be a sluggard, do not delay yourself, rise to your responsibilities and leave God to do his own.

While you are waiting for God's manifestation, God expects two things from you: **TO LEARN & TO PREPARE.**

<u>The 3 roles in the waiting period</u>

The three important roles between you and God are:-

    1. The Training role.
    2. The Learning role.
    3. The Preparation role.

(1). **THE TRAINING ROLE: -**

The first part, which is the Training aspect is the Role of God. In the training, a test or examination is waiting for you. Just as part of our Christian life journey, you should know that whatever situation that happens is an avenue to prove your love and obedience to God and it is not the time to back off.

Whether the test is from God as he tested Abraham with his son, Isaac, or from people around you or satan, you need to pass the examination and overcome as Christ has promised us victory.

God does the training through men or circumstances, while your own is to learn and prepare. Reflect Christ in your character.

God equips you and put everything you need in your life before you were born.

Your own is to prepare, pray, overcome and expect your blessing from God.

"Before I formed thee in the belly, I knew thee; and before thou camest forth out of the womb I sanctified thee, and I ordained thee a prophet unto the nations" **(Jeremiah 1 v 5)**

The other 2 things are your roles to play:
I know many of us have been praying, which is one key to our breakthrough; if you have stopped praying, continue praying until your joy is full because the bible says
"Pray without season."
Now if you have been praying but lack faith in God, you are not pleasing God, Put your trust in Him. Some of us have faith but no action; remember the word of God says
"Faith without work is dead ".

Where is your action to back up your faith? You can't just be praying and idle.

As a step of your faith in God, you must take action, so I have listed out a few things you need to do to build up yourself and prepare for your spouse. Note the areas you are finding difficult to submit to God and work on yourself. Examples:

- You should learn and have Godly virtues; to help you overcome anger in marriage.
- Patience is one of the fruits of the Spirit; which you need to have in relating with your spouse in marriage, settle it with God before you marry so that you won't destroy your marriage.
- Get knowledge, wisdom and prepare for your marriage. I am not saying prepare for your wedding because marriage and

wedding are different, so prepare for your future home.

I have written a book which I will publish soon about "The Genesis of marriage" where I explained some differences between wedding and marriage, watch out for it soon.
(Proverb 14 v 1 & 29, 15 v 1).

"Every wise woman buildeth her house,
But the foolish plucketh it down with her hands".

"He that is slow to wrath is of great understanding:
But he that is hasty in spirit exalted folly. "

"A soft answer turns away wrath:
But grievous words stir up anger ".

(2). **THE LEARNING ROLE: -**

There is something you must learn from your past mistake or present situation and you must get it right this time. Do not dwell or brood on the past but you must not make the same mistake, as God will give you another chance, learn!

• Have you repented from your past sin?

• Are you ready to repent and surrender to Jesus?

• Do you trust people more than God?

• Do you trust in your understanding?

• Learn what God is teaching and learn what God is saying in your present or unpleasant situation right now. Learn and be wise!

• If you want to get married, do you know the role of a good wife and mother or do you have the qualities of a good husband and father?

You may not be a sinner but a Christian can also experience an unpleasant situation, as a Christian, tribulation and trials are part of the training to be strong but God has promised us victory even if it comes from the enemy or Satan himself. He knew it; he allowed it sometimes for a purpose but that does not prevent you from praying. Remember Job? Trust God for better things to come. Do not lose hope. Decide to follow God till the end and he will restore and reward you.

(3). THE PREPARATION ROLE: -

Prepare yourself in all areas; I mean, do something worthwhile, especially if God has given you a vision or instructions. You must discover your purpose in life.
Do you know what you were born into this world to do? If not, pray and ask God, so that you can start fulfilling your

purpose in life. Focus on the call of God for your life, discover your gift and use it. Upgrade yourself in all areas, be it physical, spiritual, emotional, or mental disposition, get wisdom, get information, and renew your mind. (Proverb 2 v 1- 7).

Do not wait in idleness, laziness, ignorance or fear.

You may need to learn a trade, go on training, go to school, enroll in online courses, Skills or Seminars, please upgrade yourself, attend marriage seminars, read marriage literature and search the scripture to know what God said concerning his promises. As you are busy preparing for your future and making a positive impact, God may decide to surprise you with your Spouse when you don't even expect it!

I received the inspiration to write this book in the year 2000 after I gave my life to Jesus. I was compiling it little by little from the year 2000 till the year

2004 and I abandoned it till the year 2006. I thought of completing it when I get married because I thought I could not finish it until I marry but little did I know I was delaying myself unnecessarily. I later forgot about getting married and pursued the vision that God gave me. It was at the point I let God have his way that my husband-to-be proposed to me when I did not even expect it. When you obey God and walk in his will for you, he will also work on your behalf. Let us do our parts and leave God to do his part because we cannot help God.

Think of the talent, gift or skill you have and do something about it because God gave you a purpose and opportunities are coming for you to use it.

Please learn fast and prepare fast, maximising your time.

Do not delay or wait for anybody to complete you as a man or woman before you can obey God fully. It is only God who can do that. What you expect from God will make you prepare and your preparations bring manifestations of the glory of God in your life.

PRAYER EQUATION

• Expectation+preparation
=manifestation
• Faith + action =excellent result

You can see preparation is very crucial if you want quick manifestation. Preparation provokes God's favour upon your life. For you to prepare while you see nothing yet, shows how you trust God and expect that he will answer you. The bible says *"faith without works is dead "*(James 2 vs. 17).

Benefits of Preparation

1. Preparation shows you are ready for his miracle:-When you prepare, for example, as singles, the first step is to give your life to Jesus, follow God and know his will and his ways and also to know his word concerning marriage and you are obedient to his instructions in the bible day by day, it tells God you are ready.

2. Preparation gives you an edge over others.

3. Preparation connects you with wonderful opportunities.

4. Preparation provokes God to pour his favour on you.

5. Your preparation is an act of faith in God and your expectation from him.

6. When you prepare for your miracle, you are in the will of God

and he will show up at his appointed time.

7. Your preparation prevents you from self-delay.

Therefore, prayerfully prepare and patiently wait.

Ask God for more grace, pray for His Mercy, and ask for divine help.

Believe it as you meditate on these scriptures–(Isaiah 46:31, Psalm 40 v 1–2).

It will work for you in Jesus' name. It works for me, and your own will not be an exception.

CHAPTER FIVE

HOW TO PREPARE DURING THE WAITING PERIOD

Prepare your spiritual life, physical appearance, finance, emotions, academic, mental reception and marital life.

1. SPIRITUAL PREPARATION:

If you are not born again, the first step is to please give your life to Jesus. Confess your sin and ask God for forgiveness.

If you are born again, be sure of your salvation, examine yourself daily-(John3v3,John3v16,1st Thessalonians5 v 8-10, luke21:19).

(A). Pray to know the purpose of God for your life and work in that purpose-(Hebrew 10 v 36).

(B). Discover your talent and use it for God. For instance-singing for God, teaching bible study, interceding for others in prayers, writing books, drawing Christian picture books for children illustrations from the bible, making moral value stories and so on. Do not bury your talent; use it for God's glory. No matter how little, use it, it will multiply–matthew25:14-30.

(C). Do not take any decision or step without consulting God-Psalm 16 v 7, Proverb 3 v 5-7.

(D). You must be a praying man or woman, it will help you-
(1 Thessalonians 5:17, James 4 v 2).

(E). Addict yourself to the word of God and practice it. When you study the word, check your life. What is the Holy Spirit ministering? (James 1:22-25, Joshua 1-8) meditate every word you read, listen to God, think, and apply it to your life and check:

- If there is an example to follow in that passage?
- If there is a sin to avoid?
- Look for a promise to claim
- If there is a prayer, to pray?
- Look for the commandment of God to obey.
- Look for a condition to meet.
- Look for a verse to memorize.
- Check for any mistakes to avoid.
- Is there any challenge faced and overcome with prayer?

(F). Work in God's will for your life– James 1:17 Hebrew 13: 4, 10 v 38, 1 Thessalonians 5:18.

(G). Put God first, trust and obey him.

(H). You should learn a good thing and accept correction (Proverb 1v 5).

(I). Pray for the fruit of the Holy Spirit– Galatians 5:22-26.

Your waiting period is an opportunity to learn and do all God expects you to do to make you strong and mature in all areas. For instance, in marriage, God will not want you to mess up your marriage so there are things you can learn through teachings from marriage counsellors, books and Bible before you marry. (Hebrew 13 v 4, Ephesus 5:21-31).
Therefore, learn things about marriage before you marry.

- While you are waiting, you must seek God for direction, instruction, revelation, understanding and wisdom- Proverb 4:10-13.

- Do not despise your talent no matter how small it may look, it is important, and it will multiply as you obey and know that people need it.

2. PHYSICAL PREPARATION:

Take good care of your physical appearance without displeasing God.
Your spiritual life is as important as your physical appearance. Do not be deceived. The most spiritual bachelor wants to marry a neat and beautiful Spinster but it depends on how you carry yourself.
(Psalm 35:14) says **"You are wonderful and fearfully made "**.
It is not the outer beauty that counts, beauty is in the beholder's eye. Your physical outlook will attract people, so you need to take good care of your body. This applies to single sisters and brothers. Clean, handsome men attract ladies too. Being a Christian sister or brother, is not an excuse to be dirty or rough and you expect a sister to accept you just because you said 'Thou says the Lord''? Please, do not intimidate

anybody with that word. **"Cleanliness is next to Godliness "**.

A dirty lady cannot expect a clean man likewise; a rough man cannot get the attention of a neat, organized lady. That is one reason for preparation. If you are like that, let God work through you, learn and change now God is always doing his part. You too, do your part, do not be lazy and ignorant. Maybe your spouse-to-be is watching you in one corner but he or she is still having doubts and needs more convictions because of your rough way of life. Permit me to give my little tips based on my encounters with some singles. This is not to belittle anybody but to serve as an eye-opener to help, you don't have to be the most beautiful but be clean. Am sure nobody likes unpleasant odours. Am I right?

<u>My Humble advice for Single sisters and brothers</u>

1. Wash your body twice daily. In the morning and late at night before you sleep.

2. Brush your teeth also twice. In the morning and before bed. You can also use mouthwash at night.

3. Eat fruits and vegetables and avoid' junk food'.

4. Remember to wash your armpit with a sponge and soap, and keep your armpit dry to avoid foul odour.

5. Tidy your hair or comb it well. Do not look unkempt.

6. A brilliant image is a product of good posture, carriage, and moderate and decent dressing. Invest in your appearance but be decent and not seductive, seduction is ungodly.

7. Clean your nails and toes well and keep them natural.

8. Clean both the inner and outer areas of your ear. It can smell.

9. If you have just two shirts, wash, iron them well, and be neat.

10. Wash your boxers or inners daily, do not soak for days.

11. Wash your towel at least once or twice a week with disinfectant.

12. Take enough rest after work.

13. Develop a moral sense of dressing and being neat.

14. Love yourself and the surrounding people.

15. Help others and show mercy.

16. Eat a balanced diet, it is not expensive to make, what you need is wisdom and eating in understanding.

17. Drink enough water daily.

18. Take less sugary drinks instead, and juice your fruit.

3. MENTAL PREPARATION:

Your being single or rejected does not make you less important before God or among your mates. See yourself the way God sees you and not the way people see you. Single or married, we were born to serve God and there is no marriage in heaven. Every individual must fulfil the purpose of God for his or her life.

As a single, you are a complete human being. God can use you gloriously, and you can even do better than the married in the house of God. So, maximize your single life by serving God now and doing his will.

You have a great opportunity for God to use you mightily during your single life because when you marry; you have additional responsibility to take care of your spouse and children, as God is preparing you for the marriage, let your single life count, impact lives!

Marriage is not what makes your life complete or fulfilled. It is not marriage that gives perfect joy though we need it as part of the things that give us joy. Some people are rich, married and are living in affluence, yet they do not have joy, they are not experiencing the peace of God. Some people marry but they are not fulfilling the purpose of God for their lives. This is an unfruitful life, and until they do the primary assignment God created them for in this world, all these pleasures may not fulfill them. (Mathew 3v10, Luke 16v10) put God first and win souls for Christ, many are perishing.

Jesus Christ is our perfect joy and our bridegroom. If you use the gift and talent God has given you to serve others and please God, it will fulfil you. As you are doing your part, God will do his parts.

A waiting period is a period of training and a period God expects you as single sisters and single brothers to take a bold step of faith. Start preparing yourself for both the things of God and your destiny.

Whether as a single looking for the right partner or you are believing in

God in your business, career, education, job or business, financial growth and so on. There is a test to pass to show that you are mature for it. Do something now and show yourself approved. (2 timothy 2:15).

Being single does not change the plan of God for your life. It does not make you poorer or less than your mates but you should not be idle. God is the source of your joy and your expectations. Do not be anxious over anything. God knows what you are passing through. Just trust him and renew your mind, change your mentality and think positive.

- Prayerfully remind him of his promises in his word. Let nothing distract you. Luke 12:35-37.
- Do not sit worrying, fall into pleasant prospects and vision, and act fast. Remember the 10 virgins, only 5 prepare. (Matt 25:4-11) so be wise and do not delay yourself anymore.

- Learn what it takes to be a good wife or husband, search the bible and ask God for wisdom.
- If you want to be a mother or father, learn the roles of a good father and mother, how to train your child in the way of God through the bible and Christian books, and learn how to train your children now according to God's plan so that God can trust you enough to give you those children.

4. EMOTIONAL PREPARATION:

You may be in your training period, probably because you cannot control your anger. Until you have passed several times, God may not release that miracle yet.

1. Love yourself; celebrate yourself because you are an image of God– Genesis 1v27, and Psalm 139 v 14.

2. Develop self-confidence, belief in yourself, have conviction, dreams and vocation and ask God for help always.

3. Ask yourself- **'where did I go wrong in the past?** Then work on yourself to prevent such a mistake.

4. Anger can be destructive or send people away from you as a Christian, tell God in prayer to change you and crucify your flesh.

5. Allow the word of God to sanctify you, practice the word and pray it.- Joshua 1v 8.

6. The only truth of the matter is that God is your joy. Put him first before anything you are expecting from him.

7. Read Galatians 5:19. Pray against the work of the flesh and ask for the fruit of the spirit.

8. Learn to listen more than talk- (1thesalonical 4:11).
9. Learn to forgive yourself and others.
10. Accept and appreciate others. - Hebrew 12:14

5. <u>FINANCIAL PREPARATION:</u>

1. Determine to succeed because God wants you to succeed- 1 Chronicle 4: 9-10.
2. Whatever you do, do it wholeheartedly and do not be idle or lazy and God will crown your effort.– Proverb 6:9-11
3. Be a giver–proverbs 39 and 10 proverbs 11:24 & 25.
4. Be a tither- Give 10% of your profit, salary or cash gift to God.

5. If you are unemployed, create a job for yourself, and be innovative. Prayerfully think of what you can do that can generate money. E.g. baking cake, designing clothes, bag making, what you have a passion for or your skill can generate money for you.
6. Do not despise your little beginning.
7. When you are busy, do not forget God. You need him always for you to succeed.
8. If you are expecting an enormous sum of money from God, know how to spend the little you have wisely. That will determine more from God.
9. Learn a little about accounting, money and business management to manage your business.

6. ACADEMIC PREPARATION:

1. Get educated, it will enlighten your scope in life.

2. No matter your age, you can still upgrade yourself or go to school, if you are determined.
3. Enroll in either university, polytechnic, catering school, fashion design or any other vocation to brighten your knowledge.
4. In any field or skill you are, be current, seek for more knowledge- proverb 11:27.
5. If you are a graduate and God wants you to design, ask God for more direction, for example- fashion design, or cake design and your education will help you.
6. Seek God first to know his purpose for you and fulfil it immediately.
7. Everybody cannot be an eye, if not, what are we going to use to hear? We cannot use the eye to hear, so the ear is as important as the eyes, what happens to the hand? The legs?
All parts of the body have their unique functions.

You are unique in your field or call, appreciate it and improve on it. (1 Corinthians 12:14-21).

7. <u>MARITAL PREPARATION:</u>

1. Ask yourself- 'am I ready to be a wife or husband, a father or mother? Do I have what it takes?' If not, gain knowledge.
2. Learn the practical roles of being a Godly husband or wife through the bible, seminars, and marriage literature and from couples who have a Godly Christian foundation with good fruits.
3. As a Christian, get acquitted with the characteristics of a good Christian wife and husband and also learn the pattern of a Godly Christian home.
4. I suggest that as a single lady, read the story of some characters in the bible. For instance: Ruth, Esther and also meditate on proverb 31.

5. Let the bachelor or unmarried man read–Ruth 28-16, Ephesians 25-29.

Reasons for preparation

• Preparation is important to lay a good foundation for your life.
• For God to work faster on your behalf.
• For you to know that it is not marriage that will complete you, but God.
• You can be valuable before marriage and during the marriage.
• It helps you to fit into an opportunity that will meet your heart's desire.
• What you expect will make you prepare, and your preparation brings manifestation.
• You need preparation for God to build you.
• God trains you to overcome inappropriate behaviours during this period, so you need to prepare to learn good things.

• For you to be confident and competent in your area of calling.

• Preparations allow you to be mature enough to handle your marriage or home.

CHAPTER SIX

BE YOURSELF

How do you see yourself? Perhaps you tell yourself "do I matter? I'm merely a speck in the universe". (Psalm 139:14, Genesis 1:27)

"I will praise thee, for I am fearfully and wonderfully made: marvelous are thy works, and that my soul knoweth right well".

"So God created man in his own image, in the image of God, created him, male and female created them".

We see our smallness but God sees our significance.
God created us in his image, he makes us in his likeness to recreate, reproduce, be creative and be wise and useful for his Glory. We must see ourselves

beautifully created by God. Too low self-esteem can cripple and also too high self-esteem can lead to pride. We are the evidence of God's creative talents.

Try to meditate on this (Psalm 8:4-5) and imagine yourself standing, God above with his Angels and God is placing a crown on your head. This is a mark of our position and honour. We are all important in his plans and we have significant roles to play. It is the way God sees us, we should see ourselves. I leave it for us to make the best of what he has given us both physically and spiritually.
God loves every individual and he has made everybody unique.
Unfortunately, some of us are photocopies; we spend much of our lives trying to undo our individuality. Some people want to have another person's height, figure, look or talent. Perhaps, you say "until I can sing like

Sister Mary", "I won't join the choir". You need to discover your gift, talent, skill and strength. Develop them prayerfully and wisely, asking God to help you be who he wants you to be. I am going to talk about "Be yourself "in two ways:

• Be yourself-physically
• Be yourself-spiritually

(A). BE YOURSELF - PHYSICALLY

"When I was in secondary school I hated myself, I did not see any good thing in my life until a few years later. Why? Because then, I did not like so many things about myself. The devil folded my eyes and used my friends not to appreciate God in my life as I compared myself with other girls.

Naturally, I am a tall lady. I hated my height, my legs, my wide hips, my dark complexion and other things. I was so miserable that it blinded me with the devil's lie that I was not beautiful. One of my cousins told me I was too tall. A friend told me to hit my hip on the wall to reduce it. I later discovered that I have a unique and perfect figure for a growing young lady. I was ignorant of the unique quality God invested in me because I did not create myself, only God could do that. One day, I came across the word of God in (Psalm 139:14a) and (Genesis 1v27).

"I will praise thee; for I am fearfully And wonderfully made"

"I am the image of God."

When I meditated on these bible verses, I got the understanding that the way I look is the reflection of God. Anything in me, my father in heaven has it because I am his image. So I am not a bastard. Thank God for his word and knowledge of it, I later appreciated God for how he created me. My life, my thinking, my ideas, and my reasoning changed with the help of God since that day. That is why you need to read and meditate on the word of God. Do not listen to what the devil is saying.

Are you a lady and you are looking at yourself thinking, "Will any man marry me? I am too fat, too short, too dark, and not pretty or too slim, - relax! You are beautiful because you are God's image.

Sit down and appreciate God for sparing your life, ponder on his word and Check yourself one more time, there must be one unique thing that you have that other ladies do not have. Just be yourself, do not imitate others. Be outstanding. Bring out that best in yourself. Look good, wear clean cloth that makes you decent, do a moderate hairstyle that fits your look and do not go after what is in vogue but whatever fits your shape, size, colour, face, and height. So be decent.

"In like manners also, that women adorn themselves in modest apparel, with shamefacedness and sobriety; not with braided hair, or gold, or pearls or costly array;
But which becometh women professing godliness with good works." **(1st Timothy 2: 9–10. KJV).**

<u>For the Spinster</u>:

As a lady, do not be a hypocrite, this can slow down a brother coming for you in marriage if you are living a photocopied life, you are not yourself; you are pretending and not real. My dear, accept yourself, work on your strength and overcome your weaknesses and let God help you.

<u>For the Bachelor:</u>

It does not leave Christian brothers or bachelors out. You should look presentable. If it is only two shirts you have, wash and iron them well, be clean, comb your hair and shave neatly. Be neat and present yourself well and decently. Walk like a responsible man. Do not walk in a worldly pattern to impress people; this can give a wrong impression about you.

Smartly carry yourself and do not imitate friends or anybody. Don't forget that the person you are trying to copy does not have the same shape, look, height, size, body- build and flexibility as you. So why copy? My brother, take care of yourself and be neat and clean. Wash your armpit with a sponge and soap to avoid an unpleasant smell. Cream your body and hair and comb your hair well, do not barb crazy hairstyles, and be decent and God-fearing.

As a bachelor, do not think you can just cage a particular sister with "thou says the lord" without taking care of yourself? How do you want her to be convinced that you are competent? Your spiritual life is very important but you must also take care of your outlook. You may not have a job or huge money yet but it is good you are ambitious. You can look better, just keep yourself clean and even your fingernails, and toes. Be clean, responsible and be yourself. Do not say when God has not said. It is better to have pure love and be sincere than to tell lies about yourself.

Do not boast or lie because you want to woo a lady, it will backfire. Improve your abilities and work on building a sustainable income for your family, overcome your weaknesses, follow God's divine plan for your life and God will help you.

(B). BE YOURSELF–
SPIRITUALLY

God put some talents and gifts in you for his glory to manifest through you.

For instance, the gift of singing, interceding for others in prayer, encouraging others in the Lord, visiting the sick, teaching the bible, healing, Ushering, children's teachers, preaching, taking care of widows, needy, orphans and so on.

In whatever area God has called you, do it well. Do not copy another person's gift and leave your own. Be yourself. When you are faithful in little, God will add more, remember the parable of the five talents in the bible. The one that had one talent buried his talent and yielded nothing while the one that had five talents used his own and God blessed him with five more talents. Have you buried your gift? I encourage you to rise and use it.

If you are in the choir, work on the gift and tone that God has given you, you may discover untapped potential in you when you are active. If you are also faithful in one, God may give you more. The most important thing is that, you are unique in your area, nobody is like you, be who he wants you to be. Have you read that there were two Abraham in the bible? No! Therefore you have a glorious destiny to fulfil, you have a role to play in the house of God.

Just like every part of our body is important, every member of Christ's body (the Church) is also important. Think about this: Your pastor is the eye in the church as a member of the church. Maybe you are on the right hand, and another brother or sister is on the left hand. Maybe you are the leg of that church. So there is a role for every born-again Christian to play in the house of God, and not only in the church, you have a positive part to play in your community, society or the nation.

There is a need for you to discover your gift, improve on it and make use of it for God to be glorified. Accept your calling, accept your gift and talent, and profit with it.

Remember, you are unique, but God can still create a replacement if you are not using your gift for God.

CHAPTER SEVEN

THE DEVIL 'S ALTERNATIVE

When you are waiting on the lord for a husband, wife, children, and good job, for instance, the devil is always bringing his alternative solution which you will have to discern and reject.
The devil brings his alternative when we are about to reach our divine goals. In all things, before the original gift of God comes your way, there is always the devil's alternative to make you lose the original plan of God.
 Remember Adam and Eve (Gen 3:1-24), the devil lied to them and they missed paradise, God drove them out of the Garden of Eden. I leave it for you to choose whether to wait and receive God's original or to be too desperate to grab the devil's alternative, which does not come free

but with the condition to sin or compromise your faith in God.

The devil presents a wrong partner to you before the right one comes when you are too desperate to get married and you do not care who shows up. Probably you are considering some idols in your heart, I am afraid, you may marry a stranger. (Proverb 5:3-5, 12:26).
 Seek the face of God for guidance in your marriage choice.

<u>Some Factors that may cause desperation to marry wrongly:-</u>
1. Age
2. Family pressure
3. Your mate ahead
4. Envy
5. Pity
6. Canal patterns
7. Culture
8. Afflictions
9. Lustful desires

10. Sex drive

1. <u>Age:</u>

It is normal for a growing lady or gentleman to desire marriage at a mature age and there is no wrong with it, but here we are considering when one is "too desperate". It means there are wrong motives that may not meet the requirement of marriage. Age should not only be the factor but maturity and preparation physically, emotionally, financially, socially, spiritually and even psychologically. Some tribes give out their girl for marriage as early as 15-year-old because the parents are desperate to be the rich man's benefactors. That is child abuse. If you are born again, around 28year old or 32-year-old lady, for example, you cannot afford to jump into the arm of an unbelieving man because you are considering your age. Please pray and wait for the right man.

Please note, the man may not come as a wealthy man, but if he is born again and if you prayerfully watch, there would be some virtues in him.

In summary, do not consider age as a good reason for you to marry the wrong person, even as important as age is. That is the essence of not being "too desperate".

2. <u>**Family Pressure**</u>: -
Do not allow the pressure of your parents or family members to push you into a wrong marriage. If you have found the will of God for your life, Glory to God. But if you are not sure or there is no peace in your heart concerning that relationship, watch! They may mock you or insult you, do not marry an unbeliever. It is better to wait than to be too desperate and enter the wrong marriage. Do not allow family pressure to make you miss the

will of God, pray for them and talk to God.

3. **<u>Your mate ahead:</u> -**

Some people are uncomfortable with their status right now simply because they have running mates. The people they finished college together, your classmate in school, your roommate in the university or your friends. Please remember that God designs destiny, he knew you before you were born, so everything about you cannot happen at the same time as your mates. You are all unique; you finished together, but they married before you does not allow you to rush into a wrong hand in marriage, if you are born again, definitely, God has good things for you, and you will still marry too but not necessarily the time with your mates. Your mates ahead of you should not make you too desperate and marry outside the will of God. You can imagine how that type of home will be, even if you marry a millionaire.

4. <u>**Envy:**</u> -

Envy differs from admiration. You may admire good things about other people's successes, there is nothing wrong with that. You can celebrate God in their lives and use it as a point of contact for your own to come. It is with a good heart but envy comes from a sinful heart. Envy is when you are sad when people are successful. Envy comes out of Jealousy, envy is a sin. An envious person wishes that other people's successes should have been for him or her. Envy can lead to unhealthy competition.
Do not be envious, as this can lead you to be too desperate to go into a wrong relationship or marriage.

5. <u>**Pity:**</u> -

Some men have contracted a wrong marriage simply because they were trying to pity some ladies who needed help, especially financial help. It is always good to help or empower the needy, widow and so on, But marriage is another serious thing, and you cannot afford to toy with your future because you feel the only big reward you can give back is marrying someone you don't have any conviction to marry but because of the fleshly desire. This is risky, marriage is an eye-opener, do not be too desperate to use marriage as a reward, payback or pity, pray about who you should marry, only God knows the future.

6. **Canal pattern**: -

I was told of three bachelors in a church who planned to marry on the same day, same church and same Spinsters' names. For example, Brother A would go into a relationship with a Spinster named Mary, Brother B should also date another sister named Mary, and brother C should find a third sister named Mary. **This is carnal, you are not walking with the Spirit of God.**

So the three men agreed to marry on the same day, and in the same church but what happened? Bro A has the conviction to marry Sister Mary, but what of the other 2 brothers? Are you sure your leading is from God? Following that type of worldly pattern alone can lead you astray in marriage because it will bring lust since you want to compete with your friends and this can also give birth to jealousy and unhealthy competition which is ungodly. In finding God's will in marriage, don't allow your flesh to push you to look for a lady's name that will match your friends' choice in marriage. Do you know if that lady you are choosing out of this canal pattern is a witch?

Well, as a Spinster or bachelor, do not be too desperate to marry so you can avoid marrying the wrong person. If you have made that mistake in marriage, do not worry, you cannot divorce, just continue to pray for your spouse's genuine salvation and ask the Spirit of God to help you.

7. <u>Culture:</u> -

I discovered that in my journey of life, there are some tribes or cultures in Africa that sponsor marrying early. This is good as this creates awareness for girls not to play away from their supposed husbands and start childbearing early in their lives. This has a lot of advantages for the girls. According to this culture, girls may marry from 18 years, 19 years, 22 years and so on, but the moment a girl is getting close to 30 years old, she becomes uncomfortable and too desperate to have a child with any man out of wedlock, as this to them will help them have children on time even if marriage is not forthcoming. This is where I disagree, as anyone in Christ should not commit fornication, and this also shows a lack of trust in God and too much desperation.

8. <u>**Affliction:** -</u>

This is another area that can tempt a lady to jump into a wrong marriage, when a girl is suffering from poverty, she may be interested in marriage not because she is prepared for marriage or know the will of God to marry but because she needs a man to help her out of her suffering or financial lack, therefore she is prone to be too desperate to marry and go into a wrong marriage. My dear, marriage is not like that, do not use your life to play a game of marriage, you need to do what is needful before marriage and pray for God's direction.

9. <u>Lustful desires</u>: -

Do not be a brother or sister who marries because of a desire for a car, wealth and beauty. As good as they are, they must not and should not be the criteria for choosing your life partner. Remember, marriage is a life contract. Do not be too desperate to marry wrongly.

10. <u>Sex drive:</u>

Some people entered the wrong marriage just because of their desire to marry someone who can satisfy them sexually. This is a wrong measure to have a good marriage because it is a faulty foundation.

Also, let me ask you a question, after marriage, do you think it is only sex

that can build a good Christian home?
What of other virtues?
For the Singles, God does not permit you to engage in sex before marriage, sex is honourable within marriage. Sex before marriage is fornication and it is a sin both to God and to your body because your body is a temple of God. When you sow to the flesh, you reap the reward of the flesh. In other words, some people experience pain, heartache, heartbreak, STD, infections, unprepared pregnancies and other unpleasant memories as a result of premarital sex.
If you can discipline yourself and keep watch of your relationship, the better and you will not sin against God. (Hebrew 13 v 4)

**"Marriage is honourable in all,
And the bed undefiled:
But whoremongers and
Adulterers God will judge".**

I know a lady who desires to marry a sexually active man. This lady claims to be a Christian but likes to check up on her suitor in a way best known to her. My dear, you cannot be smarter than God, when you pray and trust God, he will fulfil your desire. But you cannot get the best from God by satisfying the flesh. Put all your trust in him.

If you pick your choice in flesh and eventually get a highly active man in that area but he turns out to be a beast in other areas? Please do not choose out of your fleshly desire.

Sex is important within marriage but as a Single, do not eat the "forbidden fruit", renew your mind so that you will not satisfy the desire of the flesh. God knows how to package good things for his children.

You must get rid of the lust of the flesh and give your life to Jesus genuinely, let the word of God dwell richly in you.

BEWARE OF THESE CANKERWORMS

1. **<u>Sin:</u>** Cleanse yourself of any unrighteousness, no sin is too small before God. It can be lies, anger, unforgiving heart, not showing mercy to others, fornication, hatred and so on, check yourself.
Solution: Confess your sin and surrender to Jesus.

2. **<u>Sex before marriage:</u>** This is common among ladies but you should stop it, don't delay yourself anymore, many ladies do it with their fiancé because they believe they have the liberty since they will soon marry. No! It has some consequences even though some ladies get away by getting married, but they have already defiled the bed and disobeyed the instruction of God. Others are not lucky, they end up receiving heartbreak from the

relationship in the end because what else for the man to see after having sex with you.

Solution: Stop right away and ask for God's mercy, don't visit your fiancé or fiancée alone to prevent temptation, go with some responsible people, not someone that will excuse you to sleep with each other.

3. Dating married men or women: This is another cankerworm that can destroy your future, as a lady avoid dating married men, remember what you sow, and you will reap. As a bachelor, why date married women? Don't mortgage your destiny for money or present needs. It has repercussions.

Solution: Stop fast! Confess your sin to God, ask for his mercy, and wait for your spouse.

In conclusion, when God wants to promote you, he arranges somebody who will help you unconditionally, without sinning against him. Before the time God has arranged, the devil will stir up another person he can work through, for example, your boss may want to lure you to sin with him and when you see it as an opportunity to get a promotion and you yield to the temptation, you allow the devil to steal your glory, your birthrights and blessings.

The devil also knows that some weaknesses of men are **impatience, worry and sorrow.** These are the weapons he uses to conquer many Christians. He manipulates situations to make even a born-again Christian worry over life challenges, to be impatient and sad so they can rush to do what they should not do. So, you need discernment.

When you are born again, you need to ask God to sanctify you when you are expecting something from God. The moment you cannot patiently wait and receive God's guidance, you can make a mistake or if there is a minor challenge and you are sorrowful every moment, then the devil may use it to fight you all the time. Have determination, discipline and pray to God to help you in your weakness, he will help you and I will surprise you at the measure of grace given to you to overcome such temptations. (Eze36:23-30).

As a born-again Christian, you cannot rule out temptation, Satan tempted Jesus (Luke 4:5-8) but he overcame, he has promised us victory, and you too must pass the test. If you do not strive to pass, you are not helping yourself. Read the word of God and understand it because there is always a test to pass in your waiting period before you cross over to Canaan and it is only for the winners- (revelation 21:5-8). Do not delay yourself; face reality, many people have passed the test. Remember Job in (Job 42: 10) who did not sin against God before or during his affliction. He was determined to hold on to God because he knew God and he waited patiently, though the period was not pleasant, God rewarded him double for his losses. You can prayerfully trust him and he will restore your **blessings to you.**

CHAPTER EIGHT

HOW TO WAIT FOR YOUR SPOUSE

Psalm 40:1(a) says, *"I waited patiently"*

We have become an impatient generation, and we are in the computer age. As born-again Christians, we are peculiar people. (*1peter 2:9.*)

Though "we are in the world, we are not of the world". We must observe to do what is written in the bible. If you want to get the best from God, you must pray and be patient because God is patient. Faith is the substance of things hoped for, the evidence of things not seen. We need to wait and endure so we can receive the perfect will of God. You can receive God's promises after a test of your endurance. (Hebrew 10:36 and Hebrew 13:8).

**"For ye have need of patience,
That after ye have done the will of
God,
Ye might receive the promise".**

**"Jesus is the same yesterday, today
and forever"**

If God could answer Esther, Ruth and the rest of the people in the bible, he has not changed, he will answer you, when you read their stories, and they all waited patiently and got the best from God. What do you believe God for? (Luke 1:37)

"With God, all things are possible "

The bible did not say 'some of the things 'are possible but…..
**"ALL THINGS ARE POSSIBLE
WITH GOD".**

But can you pay the price? The price is:

WAITING PATIENTLY FOR GOD

The higher the quality of your request,
The higher the price of your patience.

For you to get the right spouse, please wait patiently for God and do the right things; discover your purpose and rise to fulfil it, serve God faithfully and obey his word, tell others about Jesus, and watch and pray. As you wait for your Spouse- to -be……

1. Don't wait in fear.
2. Don't wait in Sin.
3. Don't wait in doubt.
4. Don't wait in Idleness.
5. Don't wait in bitterness.
6. Don't wait without Jesus in your life.

BUT…………………

1. Wait for your Spouse with a glad heart.
2. Wait for your Spouse while you work for God.
3. Wait for your Spouse while you read, meditate and obey the word of God.
4. Wait for your Spouse with Faith in God.
5. Wait for your Spouse while you are fulfilling your purpose in life.
6. Wait for your Spouse with relentless Prayers.
7. Wait for your Spouse and hear from God always.
8. Wait for your Spouse with Godly character.
9. Wait for your Spouse with the right attitude towards other people.

10. Wait for your Spouse and ask for God's **help** and **Mercy** (very important).

11. Wait for your Spouse by seeking the kingdom of God first and His Righteousness.

12. Wait for your Spouse by preparing yourself to be a good spouse too.

Then other blessings (like your Spouse) God will give you, Praise the Lord! The God of "Suddenly" will surprise you when you don't expect it.

It is better to get the best from God which is without sorrow than to outsmart God and accept the devil's suggestion with regret.

Position yourself:

1. Delight in the lord and make yourself happy in him.
-Psalm 37:4

2. Trust what the word of God says about you, pray about it and confess it daily. For instance, It is *written, "the Lord will perfect that which concerneth me".(Psalm 138:9)*

3. Do not be too anxious- Psalm 37:1-4, a sick heart is a feeling of hopelessness, self-pity, moodiness, sorrow, a heart accusing God, wait joyfully in the Lord. (Job 42)

4. Keep yourself busy; find joy in whatever you are doing for God and people. Be cheerful to be with. Do not let depression take over your life.

5. Be hopeful and trust God. A lively heart is hopeful and joyful. It is the heart of Christ. Let People enjoy your company, when God is teaching you about patience, you must learn. Do not be bitter that you are single, jobless or poor, remember Ruth. (Ruth 3:18) if you are a single sister, do not run after any man, let the man come for you.

6. Renew your mind- Roman 12:2, Ephesians 4:20-24.

7. Allow the Holy Spirit to work in you, he will guide you aright. - Galatians 5:16-25.

8. Discipline yourself: - Stay away from bad friends, and terrible advice (Matthew 16:24)

9. Keep your body for your spouse, you are not permitted to engage in sex till after marriage.

10. Make sure you are investing your time into what is profitable to God and also achieving your purpose in life.

Your story will soon change to glory. The circumstance you find yourself in will sharpen you for the better. Hold on to Christ and move ahead. Do not accept the devil's alternative, it always comes with sorrow, shame, and regret because you got it out of sin, impatience or desperation. It is an exchange for an original blessing from God and it is temporary, so be careful of distractions. It may come from anybody. If you know your God, you will laugh best.

CHAPTER NINE

ENEMIES OF THE WAITING PERIOD

Some things are militating against the 'waiting period'. You need to discipline yourself about them and pray for God to help you. God also has warned us against them because they are destructive.

Some satanic weapons
- Fear
- Sin
- Temptation
- Evil desire/thought- Ephesians 2:3
- Doubt- Hebrew 11:6
- Unbelief
- Sorrow
- Worry/anxiety
- Devil's Suggestions- Luke 4:5-8
- Discouragement
- Bitterness
- Anger

- Curse
- Evil manipulation
- Wrong decision
- Prayerlessness
- Costly mistake
- Carelessness
- Ignorance
- Not forgiving

All these destructive weapons above are some of the things the devil used to conquer Christians, even born again during their waiting period. We must watch out because they come with the deceit of the devil to steal, kill or destroy your joy.

Things that can cause a delay in marriage

- Sin- (numbers 23:21, Ps 19:13)
- Unforgiving heart- (2 Corinthians 2:10)
- Immature heart- (James 4:3)

- Disobedience to God's word- (Samuel 1sam15)
- Lack of faith
- Unbelief
- Laziness to take up your responsibility
- Curses- (Numbers 23:21)
- Wrong location
- Wrong step/decision
- Ignorance
- Prayerlessness
- Ignorance of the word of God
- Satanic forces
- Indecision
- Setting unreasonable criteria
- Not using your talent/potential
- Pride
- Painful experiences
- Lack of direction
- Fear of the unknown
- Long-time career or academic pursuit
- Lack of preparation
- Perfectionist syndrome
- Family disagreement

• When God wants to glorify himself in your life-(like the story of Pharaoh and the children of Israel).

At the time I was writing this book, I was one of the waiting sisters; I did not even know the man I would marry yet; I was praying and fasting but I realized I must prepare to fulfil the purpose of God for my life for which writing this book is part of it.

During my waiting period, God trained me to be patient, humble and joyful. I learned after several years how to rejoice in all situations. It was hard initially to rejoice during the unpleasant situation; poverty, loneliness, reproach, dishonour and lack but as I passed through discipleship training in (RCCG), God opened my eyes to some things and I understood how a Christian can be victorious with Joy in his or her heart.

I learnt that as a Christian; you need joy in your heart to win some battles and access some blessings.

 Joy and praising God are magnificent weapons to overcome difficult situations. God gave me the vision to write books, and he gave me other gifts in the year 2000, which was the same year I gave my life to Jesus. I had faith in God that God was working on my behalf. I wasted 14 years of my life after secondary school with nothing to show for it. Though I came from a decent background. I used to believe that when I get married, my husband will be the one to make my life complete and give me joy. I waited endlessly during those periods but no husband was coming. I later realized that God was training me in so many things.

HOW TO HAVE VICTORY OVER THE DEVIL

Whenever your miracle is about to manifest, you need to be careful of the above satanic weapons. The devil uses them to tempt a Christian when he or she is about to receive something from God. Watch and pray.

The devil comes to steal, kill and destroy (John 10:10) he does this at the threshold of your success when you are about to receive your miracles, promotions, breakthrough, or blessing as the bible says in James 4:7b, *"resist the devil and he will flee"*, so resist the devil and stand out. Do not say people are doing certain things this way, ask yourself this question; <u>what I am about to do now, is that what God asks me to do?</u>

Do not honour people above God. If many sisters are fornicating before marriage, if you are a believer and follower of Christ, you **<u>must not do so</u>**, rather resist the devil, if some people are sleeping with their boss for promotion- you must resist because that is not God's plan and God will do it for you without your sinning against your creator.

The bible says 'resist' not pray. It means do not do it, *"run away"* from it, reject it and the devil will flee. Do not follow a man to a hotel and you are praying for him to change his mind not to sin with you but why did you go at all?

If you discipline yourself and practice the word of God, when the test comes, you can pass the test. You will see how God will surprise you. Do not exchange your glory for the devil.

Watch and Pray

1. Pray that God should give you grace to be patient and not to miss his will for you- Hebrew 10:36
2. Read the bible, meditate on it, confront the devil with it every day, Study it and God will give you direction-Joshua1:8
   3. You should be more prayerful.

4. Learn to fast and pray, pray also at midnight between 12 am-3 am or as the Holy Spirit leads you.

5. Live a righteous life.

6. Ask for the Holy Ghost baptism and pray in the Spirit.

7. Do not give the devil a place- like anger, bitterness, worry e.t.c.

8. In your unpleasant situation, confess positive things and praise God.

9. Joy–is the best weapon. Your positive confession in your situation will bring manifestation. Just believe.

10. After the victory, do not relax, pray and continue in the word- devil attack when you relax.

11. Run from sin and its temptations.

12. Always be in the presence of God to revive your life.

CHAPTER TEN

THE DEVIL'S MINISTRY

The devil's ministry is to steal, kill & destroy

(John 10:10)

A.The devil as a thief

The devil can steal your time. For instance, when you are spending your time on things that are not profitable to God or his kingdom. If you spend your time gossiping on social media instead of adding value, you are a victim of this. You should use the time you want to read your bible for the bible. You may not use your time to sin, but doing the right thing at the right time is more rewarding. The devil stole my time and some opportunities around me. He stole away my time in daydreaming about a perfect man who is coming to marry me, so I was waiting endlessly for a day I would marry before I could start something worthwhile. I felt as a single lady; I should get married first so that I could plan my life with my husband, but I was wrong because you need to discover yourself first before you discover your husband, you need to discover your purpose in life and fulfill that purpose.

Imagine, I was waiting full of many gifts and talent but I did not work towards fulfilling it because I felt was not complete and competent enough to achieve my purpose, I could not even discover the talent within me. I wanted to publish this book before now. I thank God I am still alive to see it published and blessing lives. I have compiled other books I will publish soon. Glory to God.

You don't have to wait till you get married before you achieve God's purpose for your life, God has put in place destiny helpers along our ways to assist us, so don't wait, obey the call of God.

When you obey God and fulfill his purpose for you, your spouse will come along the way and he or she will be a perfect match for you that will support the purpose of God in your life.

Don't allow the devil to steal your joy, peace, birthright, and the will of God for your life, his purpose for you, your time and your love for God. I could achieve nothing until after 14yrs I yielded to work in God's will and purpose for my life.

In editing and typing this book, I went to improve on my talent and gift. I have been able to learn cap making, Soap making, computer, fashion design, shoemaking, and other things.

I paid for online courses to publish my books on Amazon; I know the opportunity is coming to accommodate my knowledge, if you want to go to school, you can still go or learn a course. God's direction will broaden your scope. It is the amount of what you know that will make you fly. Get information, be current, acquire knowledge and accept corrections, meet the needs of your customers and be sincere in all your dealings- (Proverb 9:9). Preach the Gospel of Christ to people around you, let them repent from their sin, and lead them to surrender their lives to Jesus so that they will not perish and go to hell, this is the purpose of God for every believer to do the work of evangelism.

B.The devil as a killer

The devil can kill your talent if you bury it, you will discover you are dropping the gift and purpose of God and you are busy pursuing your shadow. That is why you must act fast and not remain idle. Whatever God has placed in your hands, use it for God and use it to serve people.

God made me a creative artist, but I was expecting admission to a higher institution to study accountancy because my daddy was an accountant, but within me, I was pregnant with creativities, drawing, designing and writing, but I didn't reckon with them because I thought they were not relevant.

There is a danger if you are not following the divine plan of God for your life, you cannot be successful. If you try to imitate others and drop your purpose in life, you will waste your time unnecessarily and blame God.

I was waiting for admission to one university in Nigeria, West Africa, and I wasted many years before I went to the Polytechnic, I was pursuing my dad's profession as an Accountant but all resulted in wasted years and effort.

Maybe God is telling you to design clothes for the people of God but you feel it downgrading. You should rethink.

It does not make you any less my dear.

If everyone is a doctor, who will sew your clothes? Who will produce our food? Who will teach? Every part of our body is important and everyone cannot be an eye, what the mouth can do, the eye cannot do. Yet it does not make it less important. All professions, gifts, talents, and work are important. Jesus also came to serve and says, 'whoever wants to be first must be a servant first.

C. The devil as a destroyer

The devil can destroy your destiny, your zeal for God, your passion for your spouse, your love for some people, your strength, your vision, your power, your plans and anything good. A lot of destinies have been wasted. Many of those drug addicts, murderers, prostitutes, and dead people came to this world with colourful destinies but with one sin or the other, prayerlessness, carelessness or afflictions, they have been silenced by the devil.

Many husbands and wives that loved each other suddenly became enemies, why? The devil is attacking marriages, good homes, and even Christian homes but with prayer and watchfulness, we shall overcome. You must look up to Jesus, the finisher of our faith.

The bible says "Watch and pray "

Hope of restoration

Has the devil stolen something from you? Killed something in your life or destroy something precious to you. Jesus the life and resurrection can restore whatever you have lost, he will resurrect what they have killed and even replace what they have destroyed or cut off.

First, you need Jesus in your life; you need to accept Jesus as your personal Lord and Saviour. Tomorrow may be too late.
Surrender to him now. If you have not given your life to Jesus,

<u>Take this step</u>
• Acknowledge that you are a sinner,
• Confess your sin to God,
• Ask for forgiveness,
• Repent, don't go back to that sin,
• Tell Jesus to come into your life and be your Lord,
• Ask God to give you power over sin,
• Ask for Grace to do his will,
• Attend a bible believing church.

If you have given your life to Jesus but have backslided, God of restoration can bring you back to him. Just confess your sin, ask for forgiveness and ask God to help you.
Are you a faithful born-again child of God? I rejoice with you but take heed,

lest you fall, watch and pray, examine yourself daily and God will visit you today in Jesus' name.
Turn to God and pray;

Pray in the name of Jesus.
1. Get rid of doubt, unbelief, bitterness, sorrow, fear, worry, self-pity, laziness, ask God to sanctify you and so on.
2. Ask God to fill you with the fruit of the spirit according to Galatians 6:22-23
3. Ask God to strengthen you and renew your mind.
4. Ask God to revive you to study his word daily, pray without season and render your totality to him.

Pray this prayer:
Lord, restore every good thing the devil has stolen from me, for instance. The joy of Salvation, Peace, Glory, Blessing, Birthrights, Perfect will of God, your vision (Mention yours).

Every talent and gift that God has deposited in my life, resurrect in Jesus' name.
Every good thing that has been destroyed or cut off in my life, my father replaced them in Jesus' name.

CHAPTER ELEVEN

HOW TO WAIT & GET THE RIGHT PARTNER

You cannot get the right spouse without God. He says 'he will have mercy on whom he will have mercy. Every good gift is from above. If you see anyone who has a good spouse without Christ, it is just by his mercy, God does as he pleases and you can't question him because he is God. Sometimes some of us face a lot of obstacles and fight many battles before we could get a breakthrough even as born-again Christians. Notwithstanding, God has a special interest in us and he sees us everywhere and allows it because he wants to use us. Sometimes he is training you to be strong, and if you can't please God, who do you have? Then you cannot afford to make a mistake in marrying a non-believer of Christ because Christ is our foundation. You need God, who is the source of everything to give you the right Spouse. The bible warns a Christian, not to marry an unbeliever. Marrying a wrong spouse can affect the fulfilment of your purpose in life. Therefore, if you need the right Spouse, you need God in your life; he is the one that can connect you and your right Spouse. So, you need to wait on God. When you are waiting for God, get rid of sorrow, doubt, desperation and anxiety from your mind, don't tolerate prayerlessness and laziness and do not sin in your heart because the devil may lure you to do what will make God turn his back against you.

But wait with Joy, faithfulness to God, righteousness, patience, prayer, and preparation. Don't be desperate to marry the wrong person.

1. **<u>Wait with Joy in your heart:-</u>**
Rejoice and think of what God has done already, remember what God has done for you, and your family, no matter how little it seems, and praise him for who he is. Ask God to fill you with a heart of gratitude and praise, and appreciate him for sparing your life till now, remember, some people have died. Thank him for what you are waiting for him to do. Never be an ingrate. Get rid of bitterness and overcome it.
Bible reference: (Philippians 4:4).

2. **<u>Wait faithfully and in obedient to God's word:-</u>**
What can separate your love from God? Is it a delay in your expectation? Are you serving him only because of what you want to get? You must love him because he is God, and he loves you first, have faith in him to do it for you, if you love God, he will test your faithfulness or obedience and be aware

of that! Be faithful in your work or service to God. Ask for grace to study and obey the word of God.
Bible references: (Roman 5:3-5, Mathew, revelation 22: 14-15).

3. **<u>Wait with a pure heart:-</u>**
In your waiting period, do not defile yourself, remember Daniel decided not to defile himself, Joseph also fled from an adulterous woman who was tempting him and he didn't fall. Decide to resist temptation and watch in prayer. Get rid of anger, bitterness, envy, jealousy, unhealthy competition with your friends, unforgiving heart and any other sin. Let God sanctify you.
Bible reference: (Daniel 1:8)

4. **<u>Wait in Prayer</u>:-**
Do not be weak. Just like David encouraged himself in the lord. Encourage yourself in the word of God

and prayerfully remind God of his promises. How he lifted Joseph from prison to be a Prime Minister, David was the last in his family but he became a king, God favoured Esther, a maid and an orphan who became a queen in the palace, and he remembered Ruth, a widow and she married a rich and honourable man and, he answered Hannah and gave him a great son, God has not changed. He cannot be mocked in your life, don't be tired of praying, claim this word and trust him. Some people grumble, complain and assume they are praying, your complaint is a waste of time, it can't bring any result. Don't give any room for the devil to rob you, pray, wait prayerfully and do not grumble. When the Israelites grumbled, they did not reach their goal. Maybe you have been grumbling, ask God to forgive you, search through the scripture and pray wisely with the right motive.

Bible references: (1 Samuel 30:6, Gen 41:38-44, Samuel 16:10-13, Esther 2:15-17, Ruth 4:9-13, 1 Samuel 1:2, Philippians 4:6, James 4:2, 2 chronicle, Philippians 4:6, James 4:2, 2 chronicle, Ephesians 6:18, 1the 5:17)

5. <u>Wait patiently</u>:-

God wants to train you in patience for him, do not be too desperate to go in the wrong way, God knows the best and he works out something when he is ready to do it, nobody can stop him so why fret or worry? He will test your patient so you can be mature and complete in God. God has been testing us in so many ways. For us to grow in patience, we must pass through a process. I will discuss this better in the next chapter.

6. <u>Wait in preparation</u>:-

Like I said earlier, as you are waiting, do something that will add value to your life and others. Prepare in all areas of your life, be it physical, spiritual, emotional, mental, marital or financial. Use the talent of God in you and he will reward you. Volunteer in the things of God if you are idle, can you support or build a home? Learn, get yourself together, ask God for direction, and get busy. If you want to go to school, go regardless of your age. If you want to start a business, don't despise the little beginning and don't wait until you have an enormous amount of money. Gain knowledge, accept correction and change, learn from others, learn from the word of God, be a woman or man of prayer, and commit yourself to God. Do good, look good, know your strength, pray and discipline yourself over your weakness (for instance: laziness, flirting with a supposed partner etc.).Believe in your mind that God is doing something. God might have finished his part maybe, but the delay is coming because you cannot do your parts. Why not start now and ask God to help you marvellously so that you are ready to obey him. Don't be an enemy to yourself. That is the worst enemy. Don't be ignorant, you have known the truth, and it is setting you free now, who knows, God inspired me to write this book because of you. Will you allow the effort to waste? Act now.

Bible reference: (1 Corinthians 12).

CHAPTER TWELVE

WAIT PATIENTLY & PREPARE JOYFULLY

Waiting patiently for God is the best sacrifice to receive the best from God. Your waiting patiently does not accommodate laziness, sin, idleness and lack of knowledge.

Waiting patiently for God is to do things requires of you by fulfilling your purpose of living, pleasing God, obeying his word and instruction and doing good to others during your waiting period. You need to be active in using your talent, skills, knowledge, wisdom and gifts to the Glory of God. That is the beauty of waiting. Rise and start preparing now, the reward is coming. What is your purpose in life? Pray and ask God.

Joy is a tool that is very useful in this kingdom, you don't have to look moody, bitter or angry because others are getting married and you are not. I know your own time is coming soon but be joyful. Your waiting patiently means you have overcome the flesh, for example, worry, sorrow, lust, pride, unfaithfulness, laziness, desperation, and wrong decisions.

As you are waiting, be joyful and prepare for your next level. You need joy as a weapon and faith with action to conquer fear and sorrow.

In your waiting, your patience will be tried and you will know whether you are faithful or not. This patience is a process every Christian must pass through. It comes in stages like a seed to:

(1) Plant (2) die (3) germinate (4) grow and bring out (5) fruits before you (6) harvest.

It is not the day you plant a seed of fruit you harvest it. Prayer is a seed, when you sow it, it is not wasted, and you harvest it. God hears but your patience is needed because God also is patient and I will illustrate it like this:-

TRYING STAGES OF OUR PATIENCE

(1) Planting stage: - This is when a man takes a seed to go and bury it in the ground that is to plant. This is the period we hear the word of God and it transforms us to be born again. This is the time God pick you and plants him in his vineyard; you need to give your life to Jesus.

(2). Dying Stage– This is when you just became a Christian and you need to work on yourself, your old self must die after planting (that is after giving your life to Jesus) your life is a seed to germinate and be planted. Your consecration is needed.

(3). Germinating Stage- This stage is when a Christian experiences an unpleasant situation, which you pass through sometimes in training. The Holy Spirit works out a new you. He breaks you down and at this stage you pass through some test, if you fail, you repeat the test.

(4). Growing Stage –this is the time you grow in the word of God, you are comforted and edified, you are corrected, you gain knowledge, nourished by the Holy Spirit and you overcome temptations and other things. You can overcome temptations.

(5). Fruits bearing Stage -this is the period of maturity where you manifest faith, Christ character, and Godly virtues are vivid in your life. People know you are a child of God without telling them. It is a period of preparation for harvest and at this time you allow the Holy Spirit to have His way in your life at all times. You manifest the fruit of the Spirit. (Galatians 5:22-24)

(6). Harvest Stage -after passing through this process and you have passed the test of faith, this time God can hand over to you whatever you asked for because it is not based on ulterior motives, he has trained you, tested your faithfulness and motives. This is the period of maturity where you can receive a lot from God. Though as children of God, we are still learning every day, this is not the final testimony, we grow and gain knowledge in other experiences of life but it requires your patience. Your perseverance must finish its work so you may be mature and complete in him not lacking anything, wait patiently and trust God.

Bible reference: (James 1:2-4).

Preparation is the key

In conclusion, your part is your preparation, God will surely fulfil his part, do your own. When an opportunity comes to you and you are not prepared, you will lack confidence, you would not be competent and you can miss the golden opportunity to rise to the throne. Discover your purpose in life, use your gift, talent, knowledge, wisdom and skill, and let it not be idle anymore. Do not fold your arms. Prepare with Joy in your heart.

NATURE'S TEACHING ON WAITING:-

God has been teaching us how to wait right from our conception till we get old in all areas of our lives. Not all delay is satanic. Waiting involves a process to achieve your goal or manifest your heart's desires.

The followings are other natural areas God is teaching us waiting and patience:-

- **Waiting in Farming**: -

God has been teaching us to wait in the process of agriculture, it is not the day you plant a seed of fruit you harvest it. Secondly, it teaches us patience in waiting. There is a time for you to plant, a time to wait and a time to harvest the fruits, it is natural but nature is teaching us something.

- **Waiting In education**:-

If you are a student; it is not the day you sit for the university exam you receive the admission letter, it takes some time for you to prepare to read, pass the exam, wait for the result to come out and wait for the admission letter. So it is in your waiting, that you prepare for the new environment, the school fees, the book you will buy, the accommodation you want, and time to get familiar with the school environment. You just can't fold your arm and not prepare for the examination. So preparation and waiting are necessary because you want to experience something new.

- **Waiting for marriage:-**

There is a time for a single brother and sister to wait in the face of God before they enter into marriage.

<u>As a Spinster</u>, if God has revealed your partner to you and you are convinced about the brother, there is a time to wait in prayer and preparation and let the brother be led by God. Wait for the brother to propose. Don't go ahead as a Christian sister to propose. It is not decent.

"Whoso findeth a wife findeth a good thing and obtaineth favour of the Lord "(Proverb 18:22 KJV)

If you are sure that God has revealed the man to you, pray and inform your pastor to counsel you and pray with you.

God is teaching you to wait during this period, so be careful. Remember Ruth found her husband (Boaz) but her mentor (Naomi) told her to wait in (Ruth 3:18). As a single Sister, if you have received a revelation from your future husband, there is a need to wait, Christian Sister, don't be too eager to propose to a brother. Be disciplined, and let God do his work as you pray, he will open his eyes to see you, God will perfect it by convincing the brother too. The extent you can do is to pray about it and tell your pastor.

<u>**As a bachelor,**</u> if you've found a good thing (a sister you like), do wait! Seek God, let him lead you and give you directions and wisdom. Don't just judge a sister only by appearance. There is a need for waiting and prayerful preparation to win her after God's direction, not by seduction or deceit. In addition, as a brother who is ready to marry, get yourself a source of income, no matter how small, don't despise your little beginning. Get an apartment, don't just use a sugar-coated mouth to cage any lady and don't blaspheme with "thou says the lord", don't intimidate anybody with that. Be plain, truthful and wise. When you approach any reasonable sister for marriage and allow her to be personally convinced.

There are different ways to know if the lady is the right person, one of them is true love in your heart and there is no crime in loving someone but you need to allow the Holy Spirit to lead you and later tell your pastor to counsel you, another sign is peace of mind because there is no fear in love.

In summary, there are a lot of examples of "waiting" in all areas of our lives. We can now conclude that waiting has been part of humankind from conception till now. So why worry, why fret, why doubt? What are your expectations? God is able; he can give you the best if only you can pay the price of waiting- patiently.

Are you patiently waiting? Have you compromised by eating the forbidden fruit? Thinking you can access a suitable partner by sleeping with him or her? Do not spoil your testimony, avoid sex before marriage, and do not visit your partner alone. (Hebrew 13 v 4 NKJV) says;

"Marriage is honourable among all, and the bed undefiled, but fornicators and adulterers God will judge. "

Fornicators are singles who engage in sex before marriage, the bible encourages us to marry and not sin by sleeping with each other before the marriage whether with the right spouse or with the wrong person, wait until you marry. Every spinster has a bachelor to marry.

"The higher the quality of your expectation the higher the price of waiting, and you must prepare and pass the test"

Don't fear, don't allow the devil to rob you anymore, ask God for more grace to wait for the best but in the course of waiting, achieve something tangible in your life. Love God for who he is and not because you want to receive from him, he cannot change. Remember, the waiting period is your training period to learn good things and prepare to do what God destined you to do in life for him to release his blessing upon you.

So, enjoy your waiting period and take necessary action, there is hope for you that is why you are alive. Visualize your expectations and let them give you Joy and God will surprise you soon. Is it a husband you need -imagine yourself being addressed as Mrs. "God is wonderful" After waiting, you will bless God for giving you the grace to wait for the best. Adam could have accepted one of the animals as a wife or companion but none of them was suitable. He waited for the best and God provided a helpmeet; What if he had accepted one of the animals as a wife and didn't wait for God to take her from his rib? Consider that, (Genesis 2:19-25). It is the blessing of God that last without sorrow but don't be proud, don't look down on anybody but a God-fearing Spouse is worth waiting for And for you to receive a Born again and God-fearing Spouse, you have to be born again and God-fearing for you to be qualified.

"The higher the quality of your expectation the higher the price of waiting, and you must prepare and pass the test" Don't fear, don't allow the devil to rob you anymore, ask God for more grace to wait for the best but in the course of waiting, achieve something tangible in your life. Love God for who he is and not because you want to receive from him, he cannot change.

Remember, the waiting period is your training period to learn good things and prepare to do what God destined you to do in life for him to release his blessing upon you.

God gives his blessing without adding sorrow, but don't be proud, don't look down on anybody but a God-fearing Spouse is worth waiting for And for you to receive a Born again and God-fearing Spouse, you must be born again and God-fearing too.

The waiting period is the training, learning and preparation period where you can build your life and marriage on Christ's solid foundation. Wait for God; be taught by his word, Get trained by good a counsellor or coach in your talent, learn fast and prepare effectively. Psalm 27 v 14 says:

"Wait on the Lord:

Be of good courage, and

He shall strengthen thine heart;

Wait, I say, on the Lord "

CHAPTER THIRTEEN

MY TESTIMONY AS A SPINSTER

I started compiling this book in the year 2004, despite my unpleasant situation, The Holy Spirit was still helping me to preach the Gospel, render services to God and treat people well. The gift of writing started manifesting and I was writing something down through the inspiration of the word of God, I didn't know he gave me a gift to write books to bless his children. He dropped a wonderful gift in my life, he brought me out as light out of my darkness. There was a time I wanted to travel to another city in my country but I could not have a small change for transport. Eating three times a day was a problem. People ceased to help me. I had a delay in many areas.

One of our family friends, a married man who separated from his wife, proposed to marry me so that he can take care of me. He wanted to furnish a shop for me, and buy a car for me. He had already rented a self-contained apartment for me to stay in, but I refused. I knew he was sincere about marrying me because he had the money and he liked me and other things he promised to do. But I was determined not to compromise because I knew he had no understanding of the word of God and I believe my husband will come soon but the devil wanted me to make mistakes because of my needs so that I can marry the wrong person. I rejected the offer and preached to him to go and settle with his wife, I also advised him to divert the love he claims to have for me for his wife because that is the instruction of God for him that a man should love his wife. (Ephesians 5:25) I knew it was not the will of God for me to destroy another woman's home because of luxury.

An old friend also phoned me from London because I was in Nigeria. He promised to bring me to London provided I say 'yes' to his marriage proposal to me. I could have deceived him to escape the abject poverty but I could not do such a thing, because I will only delay myself. So I said plainly: No! Why did I say that? I am a born-again Christian and the word of God says we should **"not be yoked with unbelievers "**. If you are a believer, you are not permitted to marry an unbeliever as a Single lady or man and secondly "all that glitter is not gold" I wanted a good Christian home where Christ is the foundation even though I needed the luxury but I didn't want to marry a wrong person, so I said to myself:-

No 1- This guy is handsome but not born again and I don't know what he is doing overseas.

No 2- I will not allow short-term pleasure to deny me of long-time enjoyment from God. So I said no! I would wait for my God, he is faithful; this is one of the devil's alternatives to deprive me of God's original blessing. Even though I was passing through an unpleasant moment, I said to myself "I will wait".

"Pleasure from men can turn to pressure

But only God can give you pleasure

And turn you to be a flavour to men,

When I looked at the 14 years of my life after secondary school. My academic, marital and finance was nothing to show. I was the firstborn of a family of five, our father died in 1994, and nobody to help. But there was one thing; I kept thanking God for his protection over me and my family. Another thing is my spiritual life; I was saved in the year 2000. Since then I have been making progress spiritually. But yet other areas remain the same but I knew God can compensate me in all areas I experienced delay because God has not changed. After I finished the compilation of this book, I waited for it to be published in the year 2006, four years later (November 18, 2010) the man God prepared for me came to me on my birthday!

I also prepared and waited for God by His Grace. This book you are holding is one of my preparations because God wants me to write and I have been compiling it since 2004. Also, I've learnt a series of creative arts because that is God's purpose for my life. God will help me to establish very soon, what is your plan? Though I wanted to publish this book before now, I had negotiated the payment with a publishing company some years back but it didn't work and I kept it back with some other distractions along the way. I delayed it but God knows the best. I will still thank him, probably as I had a delay before I married, I also had a delay before I could get pregnant, and maybe God wants me to minister to both the Single and the Married who are having some delay in childbearing.

Allow the Holy Spirit to work in you, ask God for his purpose and follow it, get something doing and discover your talent and use it. Whether it is convenient or not, I made myself happy as I was compiling this book.

Peradventure, you've been preparing but you are not born again, confess your sins, accept Jesus as your Lord and Saviour, and live a righteous life.

If you are born again, Spirit-filled, and you are prepared but you cannot wait. Please don't allow the devil to rob you of your birthright because of anxiety or lies of the devil. Remember Esau, because of food he could not bear his present situation at that moment; he sold his glory and blessing. (Genesis 25:29-34).

He despised his birthright, oh! What a pity! He missed it, something that could not be retrieved. Please wait for your turn, wait for your husband, wait for your wife, wait for your divine children from God and wait for your promotion to come from God.

Wait in prayer, prepare to work, Isaiah 60 v 1 says **"Arise and shine"** prepare to dress well, prepare to start a small business, don't be a liability but be an asset, wisely invest in your time, manage it well for something that will yield a positive result. Gain knowledge. Sister, don't think it is only marriage that will complete you or change your situation. Every man prefers an asset, not a liability. Even if God has destined you to marry a rich man, don't be idle. Be a virtuous woman, learn from her. (Proverb 31:10-31) Discover your purpose in life and fulfil it.

Brother, work or start a business, don't look for a rich woman to marry because of your situation. You are supposed to be a provider of the home and the head even if your woman is rich. You must still provide to obey God and receive his blessing. You can cry to God to help you receive his blessing like Jabez.

Take action now; start small, dream big and grow fast. Don't sell your birthright to a woman. Even though she is your supporter, a helpmeet, don't wait for her to come before you can work. Do a Godly job or business. Go to school if you want to and God will crown your effort. If you want the best result

- Be qualified- be born again

- Be prepared- get busy

- Wait- pass the test

Some waited but were unprepared, and some people prepared but were not qualified, only those who are qualified, prepared and waited are wise. Are you born again?

Set a plan for yourself, what you want to achieve every day and manage the time wisely because there is no time to waste anymore, don't just sit there because a prophet has said good things to you. You have a part to play. Elijah had received a revelation of abundance long again but he didn't sit down there, he prayed until after 7 days when the manifestation came (1 king 8:41-46).

"And from the days of John the Baptist until now the kingdom of God suffered violence and the violent take it by force". - Mathew 11 v 12. (KJV).

Joseph also faced trial, but he passed. He refused to commit fornication with Portifah's wife because he feared God; he didn't want the devil to steal away his glory because of three minutes of pleasure, some people would have seen such often as 'free blessing'. Many times Satan has used it to steal away some glory. Singles please be warned: being single does not change the plan of God for your life, don't be distracted, don't be discouraged, and don't be tired. I have experienced poverty, loneliness, lack of money, stagnation, satanic oppression and dishonour, But I thank God for today.

God led me to read the story of Esther on October 18, 2000.

I learnt that Esther was a deliverer of Israel, an intercessor; she brought deliverance and salvation to her people. Thank God today; I have compiled other books apart from this. I was single when I compiled these books. I was still not married. I completed the editing of this one when I got married. I later did the final editing, proofreading and publishing.

God gave me a new name. Like he changed some peoples' names in the bible".

(A). Abram was changed to **Abraham**

(b). Sarai was changed to **Sarah**
(c). Jacob was changed to **Israel**
(d). Saul later changed to **Paul.**

Ask God to give you a new name. Name we bear matters, do you know the meaning of your name? If yes and is it glorifying God? But if it is glorifying Satan, please read the story of Jabez. As a single lady, I got saved in the year 2000, 1 prayed and waited for 10 years before I married but I would have loved to marry at age 25. I was afraid to clock 30 years before I marry but behold, I married about five days to my 36 years birthday, I thank God I had not married before now, if not maybe I would have messed up the marriage because I wanted to get married as early as 25 years old, but I was not equipped to know how to build a Godly Christian home. I remember five years after I got born again; I was faced with diverse temptations and distractions, and even backslid as a young convert, but the most important thing was that I realized it on time and acknowledged those sins, confess them and was restored to God, after that, I trusted God I knew he had a better plan for me if only I could pass the test and overcome temptation, which I did by his grace. I am determined to wait for God to give me my desired matrimonial home. Though I didn't know who my husband was I didn't just approve of any man be it a drunkard, smoker, or unserious man to think I could change him. Adam did not call any of the animals his wife and God saw his needs and met them. What if Adam had called a lion or bird his wife because of loneliness, who knows what would have happened (Genesis 2:20) so God gave him the bone of his bone and the flesh of his flesh who is compatible with him, a woman he loves, his helpmeet (Genesis 2:22-23) I knew that God will also do it for somebody reading this book very, very soon in Jesus name (Amen).

Although my heart wanted to love and be loved, I wanted to experience the joy of marriage. I settled it with God in prayer to help me wait for His perfect will for me because it will be heartbreaking and disastrous to get married just to anybody because of anxiety. I faced many discouragements, pressures at home, and pity from loved ones. Some people loved me to the extent they wanted to matchmake me with a man, but I told them joyfully that I am not an object of pity and my God is bringing me to my own soon.

I confessed positively, and God answered my prayer because I believe in God although with a humble heart, I wanted a God-fearing man who loves God and he did it. Your confession also matters during this period.

Please note, that the right person cannot be measured by financial status, academic standard, or family background though they are important but by a man or woman who fears God and loves God. As a born-again Christian, Do not be unequally yoked, so why think of marrying a non-believer? Don't think you can change him or her. Build on the word of God, not by your reasoning.

Only God can convert souls, don't think you can marry someone and change him or her. Let God lead you, but do not cast an idol in your heart. It is good to have some qualities in mind but be flexible, the first thing to check is a genuine believer of the word of God and a true follower of Christ, not a pretender!

As for me, I did not want to rush into error for the sake of meeting up with my mates that were far ahead of me and also because my younger ones around me have married before me. For as much as I desire to marry quickly but it was not in my own making to do so as I feared laying a wrong foundation, I wanted a home with Christ as the Landlord where I and my hubby will follow the pattern of God.

I have compiled other books alongside this that I will be publishing soon. To God be the glory, my man showed up on November 18th, 2009, he is someone I knew as a casual friend. I mean where I was working as the company Secretary, he happened to be one of our Clients, I had been seeing him but never thought he was the man I would marry.

The surprising thing was that exactly on my birthday, he defined the relationship. I remembered I asked God to give me my Spouse as a birthday gift. We got married a year after he proposed, precisely, November 13th 2010.

I pray for you Sister, that you will not miss your divine husband in Jesus' name (Amen).

I pray for you brother, God will open your eyes to see the bone of your bone and the flesh of your flesh, and also provide the resources you need to be the man in your home in Jesus' name. (Amen).

I will conclude here....

If you see yourself going back or you have not surrendered to Jesus, today God is waiting for you, why not pause now, acknowledge your sin, confess to God now and give your life to Christ? Ask Jesus to come into your life and restore you to him. He is ready to help you. He will give you a brand new life. Shalom!

CONNECT WITH ME

Thanks for purchasing this book. I would like to hear your testimonies. You can contact me at this email: wisebrandmedia@gmail.com

Also for prayer, counselling, update of my new books, or if you have testimonies to share, you can download the Telegram App and type the telegram address below to join my telegram group so we can still communicate together.

Love from me.

You can join my Telegram group for the Singles:

https://t.me/WaitingSingles

You can also follow me on my social media platforms below:

instagram.com/estheratoi

twitter.com/EstherAtoi

facebook.com/AtoiEsther

Please Like our Facebook page: https://www.facebook.com/digitalLiteratures/

Website

Blog post: https://relationshippills.blogspot.com

Get a copy of "Waiting Singles" magazine and other books here

I NEED A FREE COPY OF WAITING-SINGLES MAGAZINE

OR click here for a free magazine

SUBSCRIBE TO OUR YOUTUBE CHANNEL

ABOUT THE AUTHOR

Esther Atoi has been a believer and follower of Christ since the year 2000. She is happily married. She studied Petroleum Marketing Technology at Petroleum Training Institute, Nigeria.
She is a writer and a creative designer. She has a passion for Singles and Married people who are experiencing waiting periods.
She loves to serve God and please him by spreading the gospel of Christ.

ABOUT THE BOOK

This book **" How to Wait & get the Right Partner "** will help Bachelors, Spinsters, unmarried moms, young widows or widowers who desire to get married.

It explains what you need to do as you are waiting for your Spouse-to-be and avoid unnecessary delay if you desire a Godly Christian home and want to fulfil God's purpose in your life.

It will give you an understanding of what happens during your waiting period and opens your eyes to the solution to getting the right man or woman to marry with personal testimonies from the Author.

NOTE

NOTE